Breheimen

A Solo Female Wanderer Hiking Guide

Breheimen, A Solo Female Wanderer Hiking Guide. Copyright 2024 by Sarah Rowe. For more information about this hiking guide and others, email hi@solofemalewanderer.com

ISBN 978-1-961878-07-5 for paperback

Introduction

Breheimen may be my favorite national park in Norway. It feels like a Norway in miniature - starting near the fjords and then climbing into the high mountains, surrounded by glaciers. It's some of the most spectacular nature that Norway has to offer, as well as some of the most challenging hiking.

I first experienced Breheimen on my 350km Massiv hike in summer 2022, and I loved it so much that I went back two years later to spend more time exploring the area.

Like many places in Norway, the best way to experience Breheimen is through cabin to cabin hikes, utilizing the cabins run by the Norwegian Trekking Association (DNT).

Table of Contents

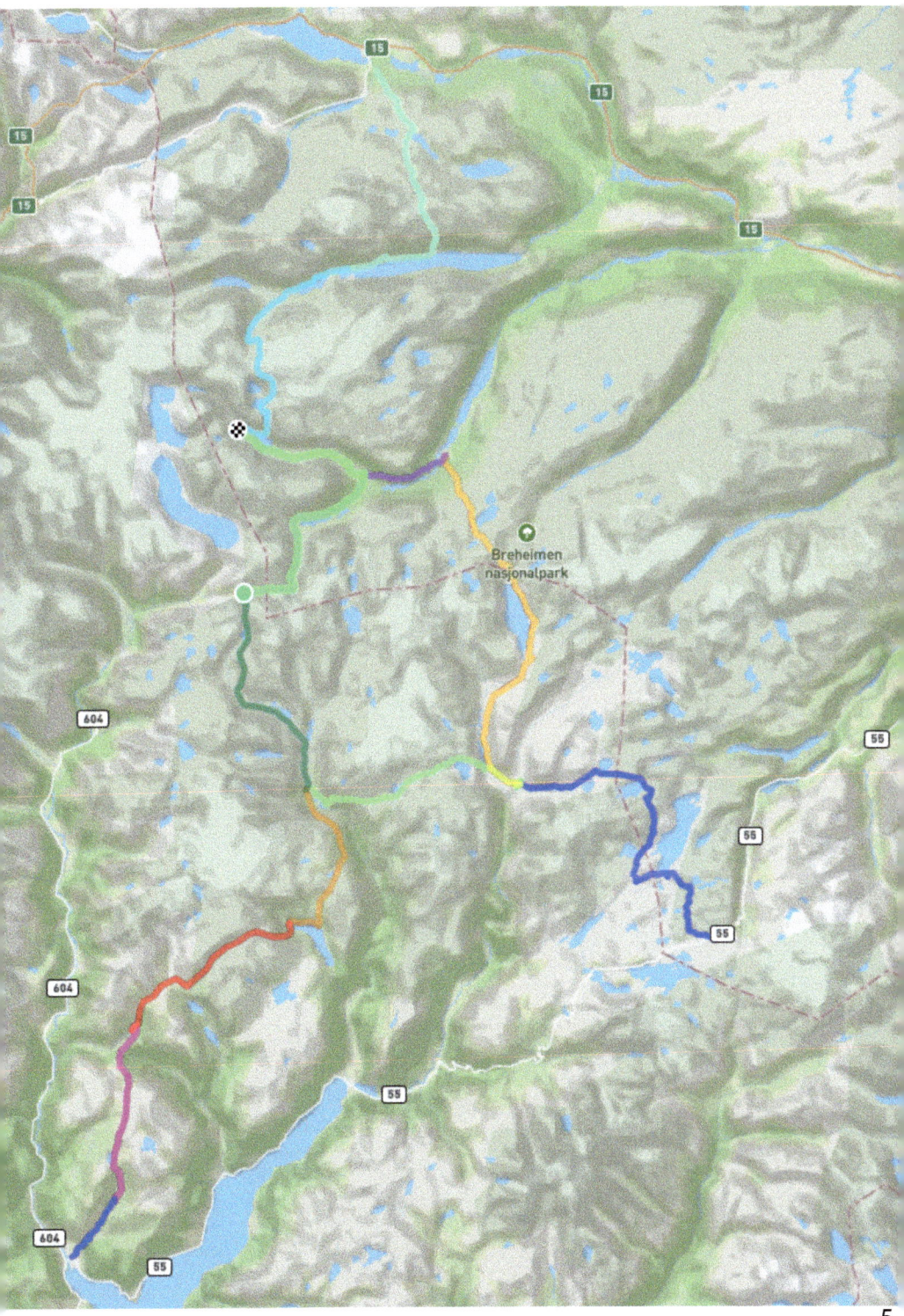

Recommended Routes

From Fjord to Fjell (From Fjord to Mountain):

This hike is a five day trip and only 61km, but the elevation gain is intense - more than three thousand meters. It's challenging terrain, too, with rocky high mountains, steep ascents and descents, spots of bog ("myr" in Norwegian), and snowfields late in the summer. But if you get good weather, it's absolutely spectacular.

Route	Length (km)	Elevation Gain (m)	Elevation Drop (m)	Time (ut.no)	My rating
Gaupne – Navarsete	5.3	594	4	3	Moderate
Navarsete – Vigdalstøl	12.0	662	517	4	Moderate
Vigdalstøl – Fast	13.4	674	603	5.5	Challenging
Fast – Arentzbu	12.6	625	598	4.5	Challenging
Arentzbu – Nørdstedalseter	15.7	748	688	6	Challenging

Four Days in Breheimen:

If you're looking for a long weekend hike that's also a physical challenge, this loop is perfect. The terrain is challenging but spectacular.

Route	Length (km)	Elevation Gain (m)	Elevation Drop (m)	Time (ut.no)	My rating
Sota Sæter – Nørdstedalseter	25.4	1,333	1,065	10	Extremely challenging
Nørdstedalseter – Arentzbu	15.7	688	748	6	Challenging
Arentzbu – Sprongdalshytta	17.0	885	489	6	Challenging
Sprongdalshytta – Sota Sæter	20.3	376	915	6	Challenging

Massiv First Stage:

Massiv is DNT's longest SignaTUR tour and a massive (pun absolutely intended) test of mental and physical strength. It's divided into four sections through four national parks, and Breheimen is the first section – and the toughest section.

Route	Length (km)	Elevation Gain (m)	Elevation Drop (m)	Time (ut.no)	My rating
Sota Sæter – Nørdstedalseter	25.4	1,333	1,065	10-12	Very challenging
Nørdstedalseter – Sognefjellshytta	26.5	959	570	10-12	Very challenging

Day by Day Hiking Routes

Route	Page	Length (km)	
Gaupne – Navarsete	10	5.3	
Navarsete – Vigdalstøl	12	12.0	
Vigdalstøl – Fast	14	13.4	
Fast - Arentzbu	16	12.6	
Arentzbu – Sprongdalshytta	18	17.0	
Arentzbu - Nørdstedalseter	20	15.7	
Sprongdalshytta – Sota Sæter	22	20.3	
Sota Sæter– Nørdstedalseter	24	25.4	
Nørdstedalseter - Sognefjellshytta	26	26.5	
Nørdstedalseter – Medalsbu - Trulsbu	28	15.4	
Medalsbu/Trulsbu – Bismo	30	20.2	
Sprongdalshytta – Slæom	32	21.5	
Slæom – Skridulaupbu	34	17.4	
Skridulaupbu – Grotli	36	17.4	

Elevation Gain (m)	Elevation Drop (m)	Time (ut.no)	My rating
594	4	3	Moderate
662	517	4	Moderate
674	603	5.5	Challenging
625	598	4.5	Challenging
885	489	6	Challenging
748	688	6	Challenging
376	915	6	Challenging
1,333	1,065	10-12	Extremely challenging
959	570	10-12	Extremely challenging
563	219	6	Challenging
129	648	5	Moderate
473	641	8	Challenging
747	938	9	Extremely challenging
821	838	9	Extremely challenging

Gaupne to Navarsete

5.3km
3.3 miles

594 meters
1,949 feet

4 meters
13 feet

3 hours
Moderate

There are two options for this hike - either from Gaupne or Høyheimsvik. Both are similar in elevation profile and terrain.

From Gaupne, the hike starts on a blue-blazed trail maintained by Luster Turlag, which goes up along a waterfall on a very steep climb. The trail can be muddy if it's rained recently, but it's well marked. After 400-500 meters of elevation gain, the trail meets a dirt road. Turn left onto the dirt road and follow it back through a series of small farms until you reach Navarsete.

My hiking notes

This is a short but steep hike - it's a straight climb up along a waterfall until you reach the road. It's a nice first or last day for a longer Breheimen trip, though, because it's relatively easy and the terrain is smooth. I felt comfortable doing this late in the day and getting to Navarsete in time for dinner.

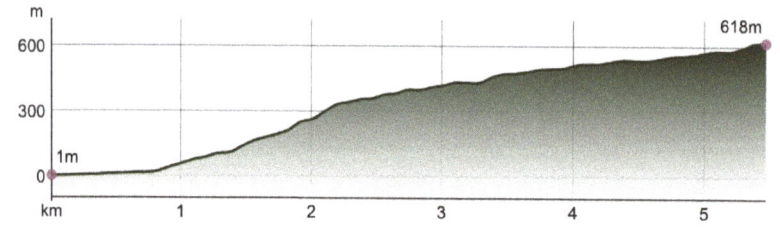

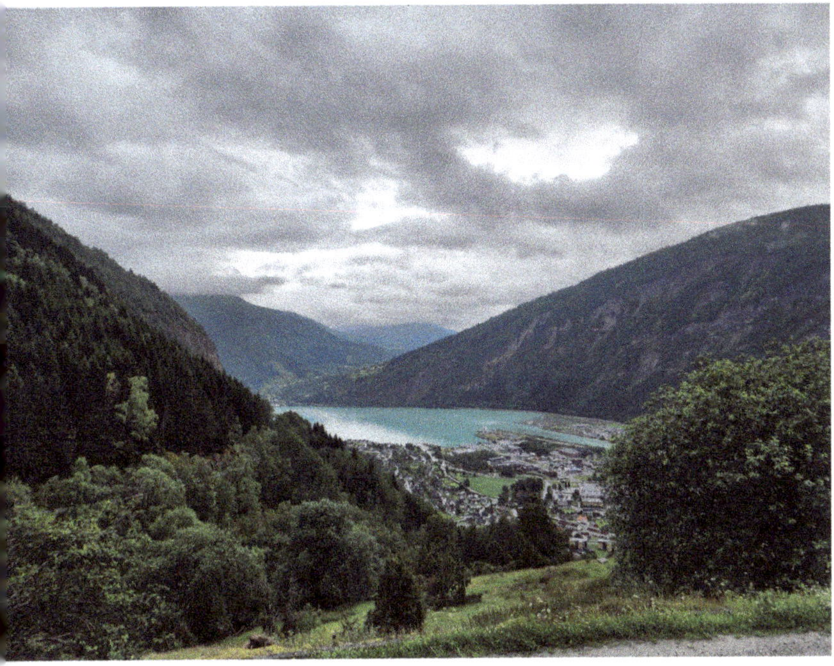

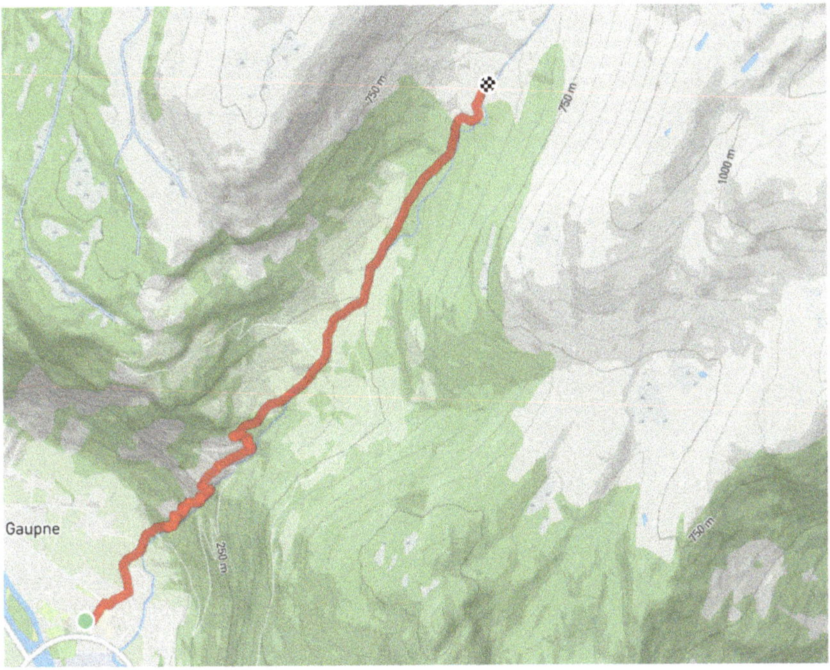
750 m
750 m
1000 m
Gaupne
250 m
750 m

Navarsete to Fivla and Vigdalstøl

12 km 7.5 miles	662 meters 2,172 feet	517 meters 1,696 feet	4 hours Moderate

Today starts by climbing up behind Navarsete into the high mountains. The first part of the day is steep, but the trail is well marked and easy to follow. The trail follows a river up to a lake. After hiking along the lake, the trail begins to gradually drop elevation, going through technically easy high mountain terrain. The route passes by Fivla, an unserviced DNT cabin with spectacular views out both east and west. The view from Fivla is spectacular, and Fivla can be a great place to stop if you're not feeling like going longer.

Once the trail passes Fivla, it's a steeper downhill to reach Vigdastøl through a birch forest. There is eventually a sign towards Vigdastøl. Turn left, cross a bridge, and then there's a couple hundred meters to the cabin.

My hiking notes

This route really starts to feel like Breheimen - there were impressive waterfalls and dramatic rock faces along the route - although there are still plenty of sheep to keep you company on the way. The terrain isn't too difficult, and there are lots of places to stop and have snacks.

I loved this hike - beautiful, not technically challenging, but I really started to feel like I was in the wilderness again.

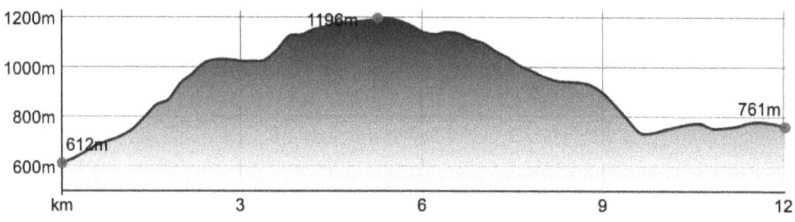

Vigdalstøl to Fast

| 13.4 km | 674 meters | 603 meters | 5.5 hours |
| 8.3 miles | 2,211 feet | 1,978 feet | Challenging |

The route starts with a climb through mostly high mountain terrain. It's a long, slow climb over mostly dirt trails. The trail passes to the south of the Hamrsdalsnosi, a peak, after about seven kilometers of hiking. The trail continues to climb up, with the terrain getting rockier. This section may have snowfields left into July.

From the top, you'll drop nearly 600 meters of elevation to reach Fast. This section goes through more shrubs and plants and can be very wet. Once you drop elevation, cross over a summer bridge over the river coming off Spørteggbreen (the Spørtegg glacier) and then to the cabin.

My hiking notes

This section was more mentally challenging than I expected. It's a long climb up from Vigdastøl, but it's a gradual enough climb that it often felt like I wasn't making any progress. I'm also not a fan of snowfields, and there were huge snowfields left in the beginning of July. I'd say the UT time estimate is on the low end.

The descent down to Fast is a little confusing - I had trouble spotting the trail markers in the plants, and it looks like there may have been a trail redone at some point recently. The good news is that you can just directly drop down to the cabin, but it felt a little bit like bushwhacking at times.

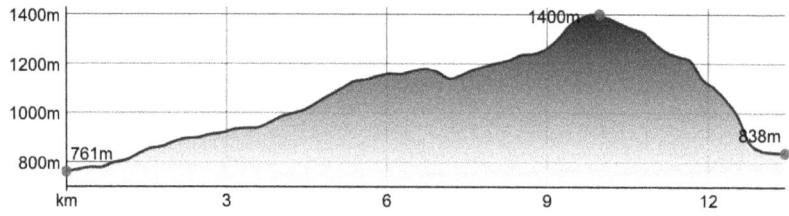

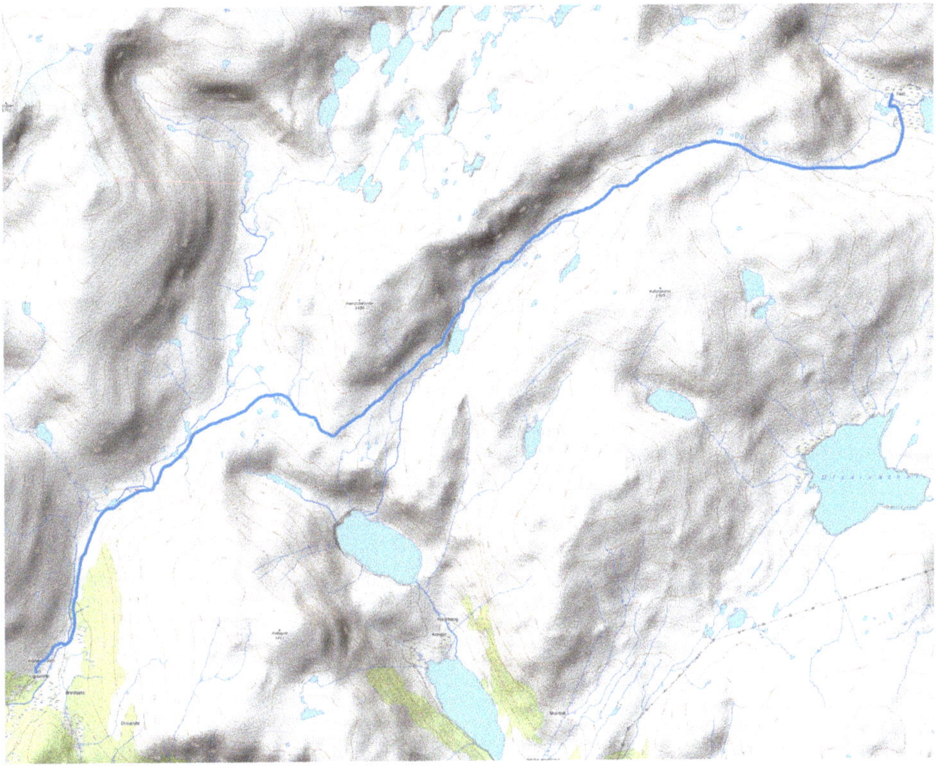

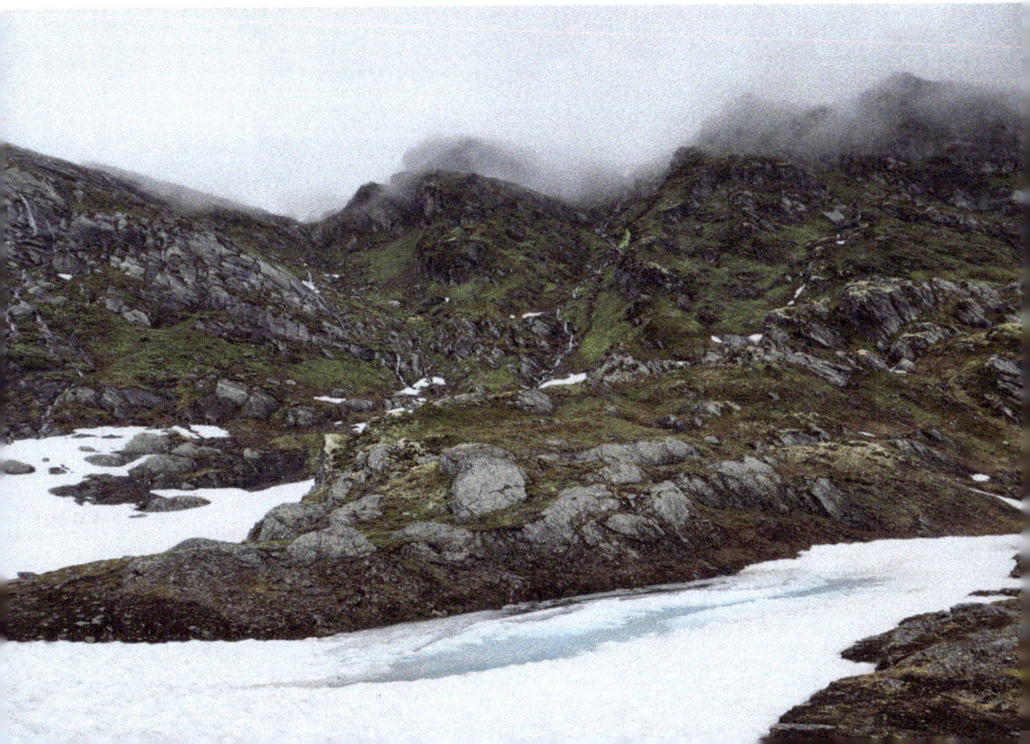

Fast to Arentzbu

| 12.6 km | 625 meters | 598 meters | 4.5 hours |
| 7.8 miles | 2,051 feet | 1,962 feet | Challenging |

The route goes along a lake, following a sheep trail between 5 to 10 meters above the lake. The trail reaches a small farm with a collection of buildings, and from here, the path turns north and starts a steep climb up. The climb gradually becomes less steep as the trail enters high mountain terrain at around two to three kilometers of hiking.

The trail passes between two mountain tops, Kolinosi and Skurvenosi, at between four and five kilometers of hiking. From here, it starts to drop gently down. The views in front of you open up, and it's possible to see into the valley with Arentzbu in the distance. The trail turns slightly more towards the west and then continues to drop elevation. As the elevation drops, the trail becomes more muddy. There's one intense drop at about kilometer eleven, then a very gradual climb to the cabin.

My hiking notes

I did this trail after a few very rainy days, and the second section was quite muddy. I had one interesting river crossing where I had to scramble across a ladder - clearly put in place because there was a sudden need for a way to get across. Other than that, it's not a technically challenging hike.

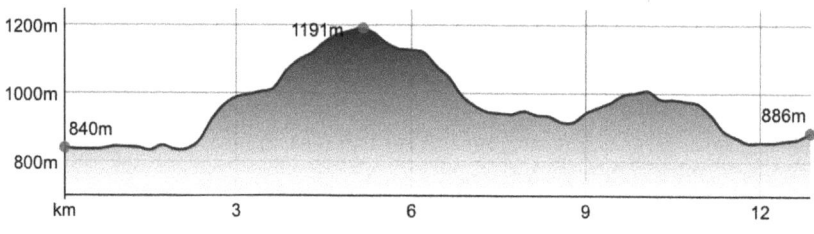

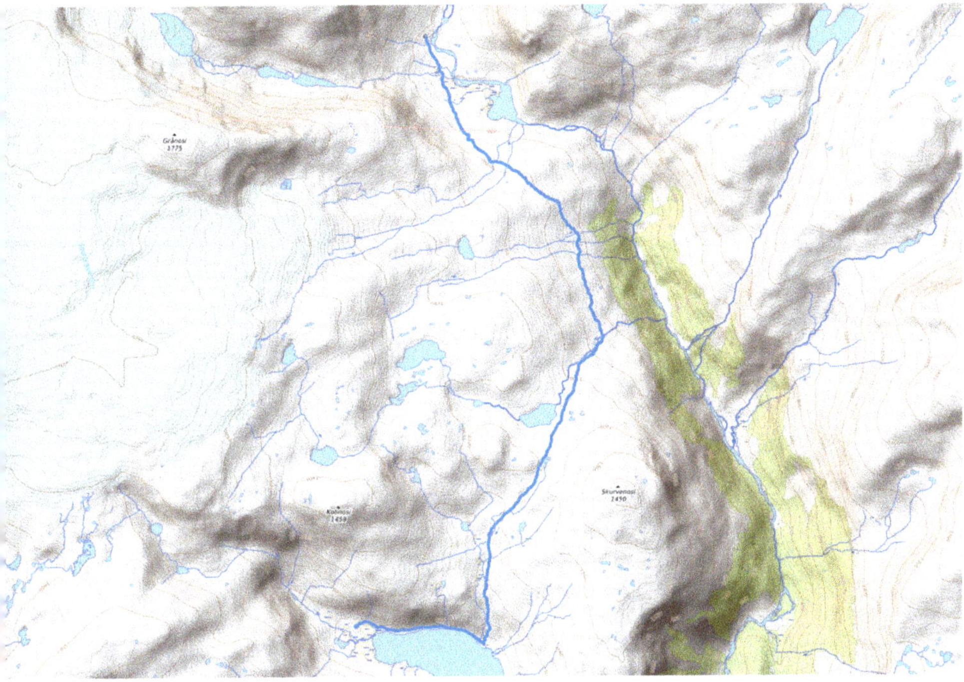
Grånosi
1775
Skurvenosi
1490

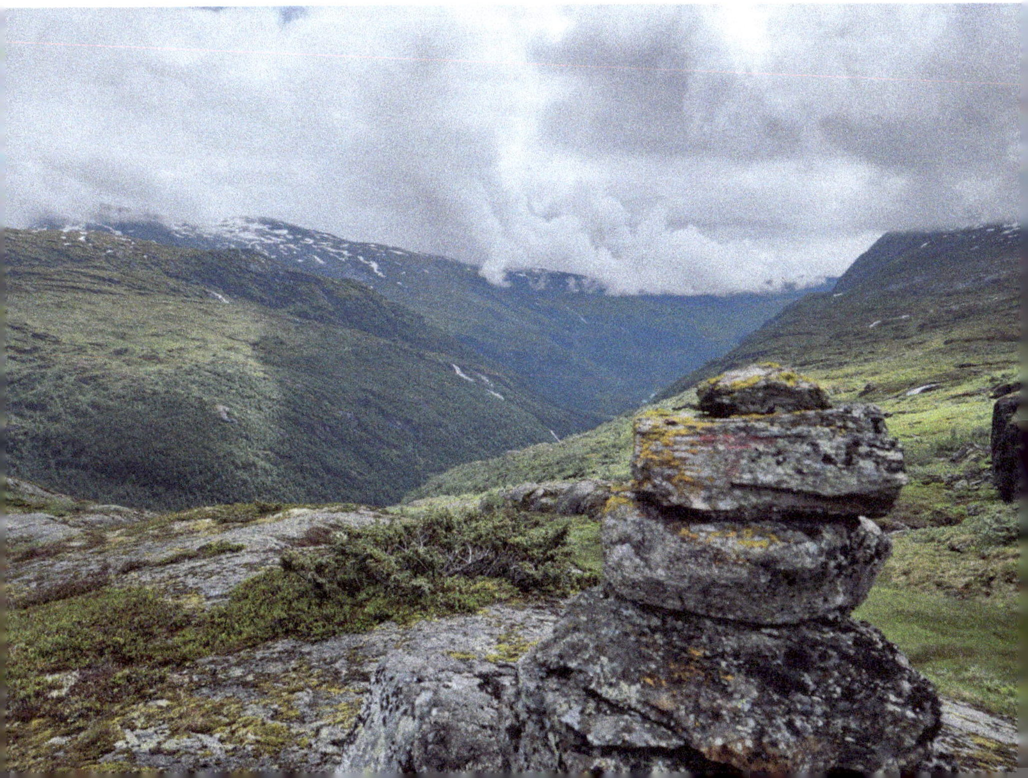

Arentzbu to Sprongdalshytta

| 17.0 km | 885 meters | 489 meters | 6 hours |
| 10.6 miles | 2,904 feet | 1,604 feet | Challenging |

Start by heading north from the cabin. The trail splits off from the trail heading to Nørdstedalseter here - make sure not to cross the bridge and instead take the trail towards the left. The trail turns towards the west and into the Greindalen ("Grein valley"). As the trail slowly climbs up, it passes over a few rivers that may need to be waded depending on the recent rainfall. The trail continues a slow climb until about 1,450 meters over sea level, about ten kilometers into the hike.

At this point, the trail becomes rocky, and there may be snowfields left until late in the summer. The trail climbs up to 1,500 meters above sea level through rocky terrain, then starts a very steep descent towards Sprongdalshytta. This section is on open rock face and can be very challenging in the rain or if there are snowfields. After descending, the trail goes around a small lake and then reaches the cabin at the west side of the lake.

Hiking notes

If it's raining, this is a very challenging hike. The descent down to Sprongdalshytta is extremely steep and slippery, and there are no handholds to help out with balance. Similarly, in case of rain, the rivers will be high enough that they need to be waded - there is no way to cross without wading. I enjoyed the first two thirds of the hike much more than the last third.

Sprongdalshytta is one of my favorite cabins, though, and well worth the hike to get there. It's perched on a rock face overlooking a glacier, and the views are spectacular if the clouds clear.

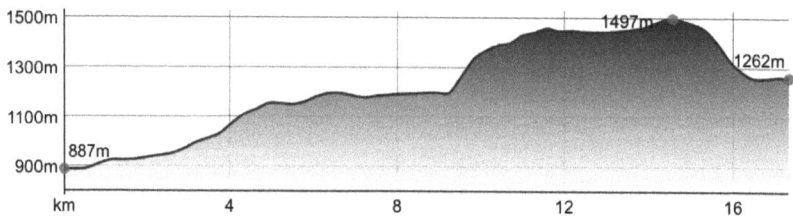

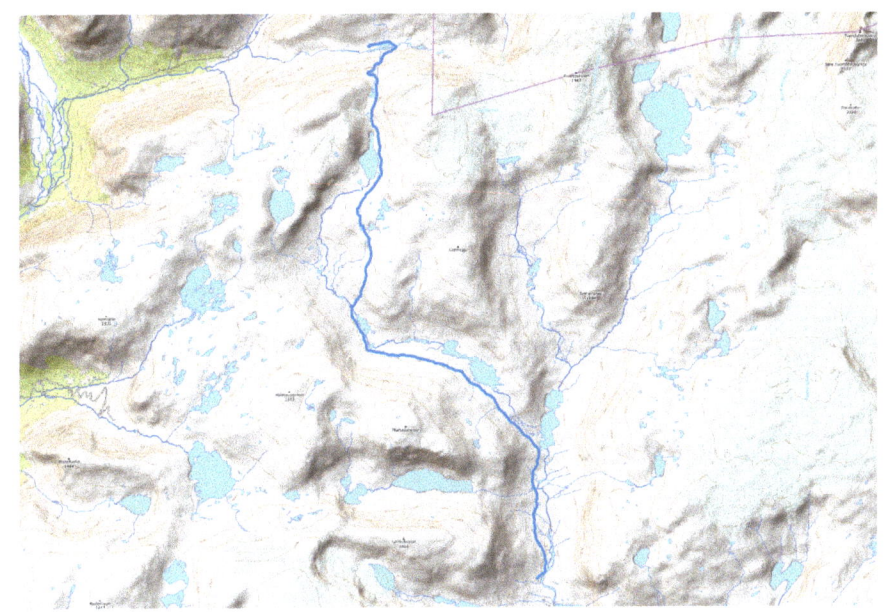

Trail conditions: very rocky. Photo taken around kilometer 13

Arentzbu to Nørdstedalseter

| 15.7 km | 748 meters | 688 meters | 6 hours |
| 9.8 miles | 2,454 feet | 2,257 feet | Challenging |

The hike starts by going over a bridge near Arentzbu, then continues through a green and often wet section to the bottom of the climb up Oksli. After this, the trail climbs steeply up before reaching a flatter section at the top of Oksli. The trail crosses over several small rivers that may need to be waded if there has been rain recently. The trail reaches Leirvatnet, then crosses over a bridge at the end of the lake, then continues on towards Gravdalsvatnet. From here, there is a steep drop to a power station at the end of a hydroelectric lake. The trail meets up with a construction road here that covers the last 2.5 kilometers to Nørdstedalseter.

Hiking notes

This section can be very technically challenging if there has been rain recently, both because of the rivers to be waded and because of slippery rocks. There may also be snowfields late in the summer hiking season. Take this one slowly. The UT estimate will be on the low end if there's been bad weather.

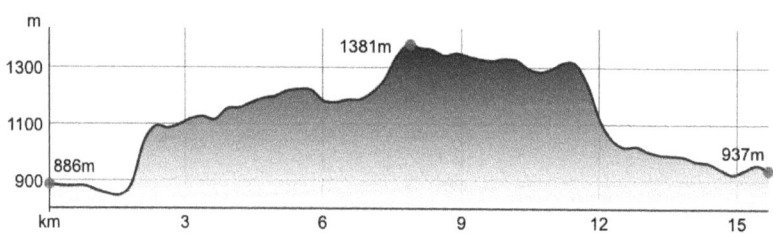

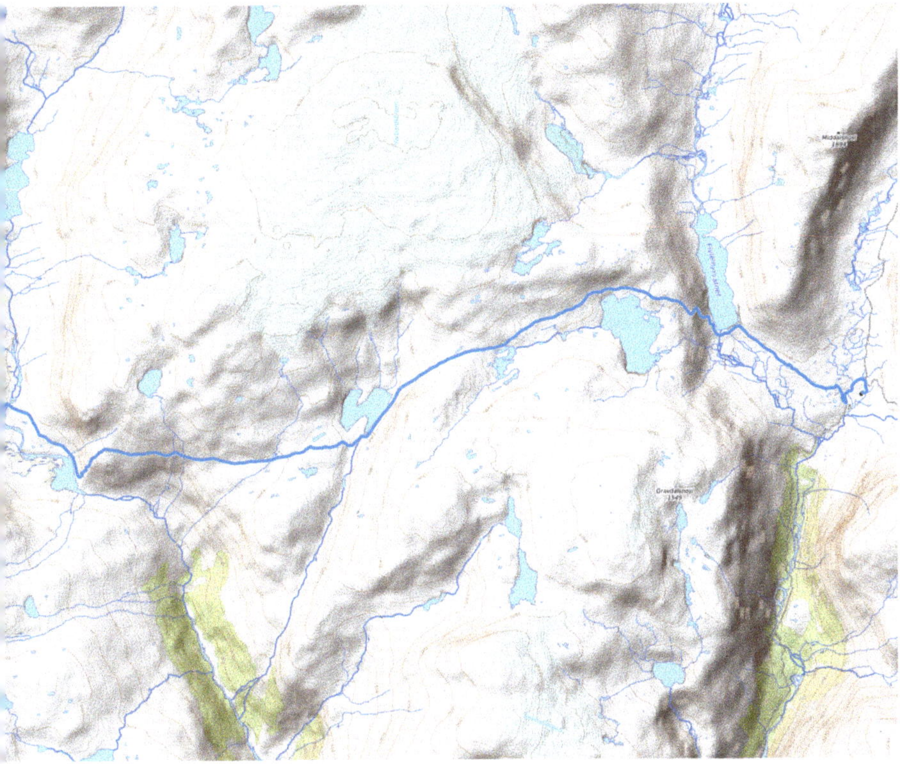

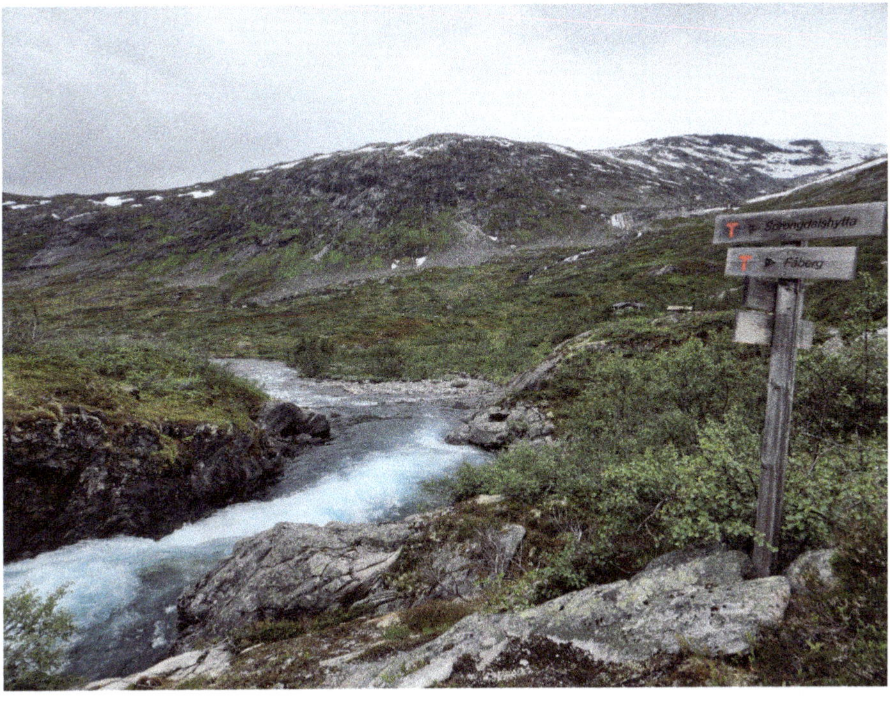
Fåberg

Sprongdalshytta to Sota Sæter

| 20.3 km | 376 meters | 915 meters | 6 hours |
| 12.6 miles | 1,234 feet | 3,002 feet | Challenging |

The trail starts by going north of the lake behind Sprongdalshytta, passing the turnoff for the trail to Arentzbu. From there, the trail climbs slightly up to about 1,350 meters over sea level before starting a descent through a bowl. It's moderately rocky through this section and can have snowfields left. The trail drops steeply down, then turns towards the north and passes by several small lakes. At about 8.5 to 9 kilometers, the trail turns towards the east, passing above Surtbyttvatnet. Continue following the trail until it reaches the intersection with the trail heading to Slæom. There is a gate and a bridge to cross here and several signs indicating the direction to Sota. From here, it's possible to either take a dirt road or a trail along the river to Sota. Both routes are about five kilometers and largely flat.

My hiking notes

Once you finish the first kilometer, this isn't too challenging of a hike. I had a little bit of trouble with it, but that was mostly because I wasn't expecting it to be so wet in the second half. If I redid it, I would take the first half more slowly and enjoy the views more.

I highly recommend taking the path by the river rather than the road to Sota. The river is quite strong and cool to hike next to, and the path feels very much like it's in the wilderness despite being so close to the road.

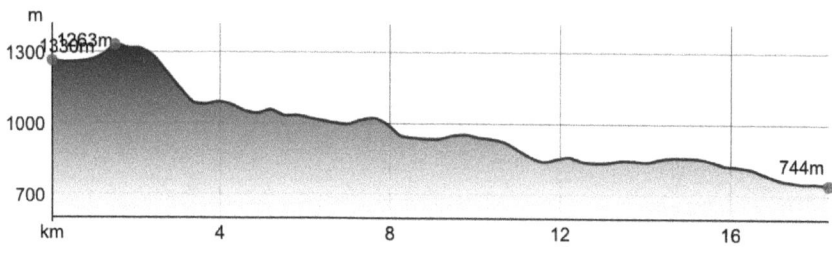

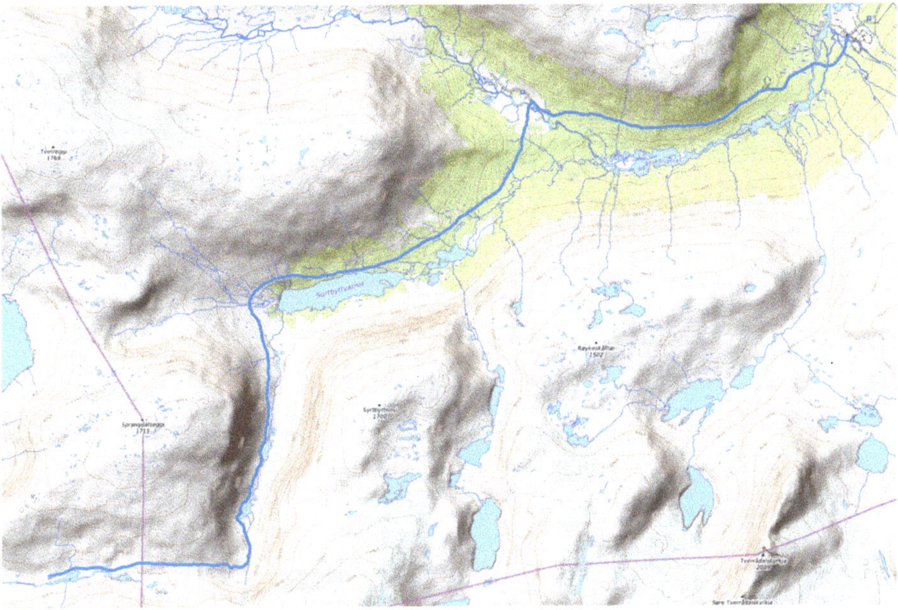

Conditions went from very rocky to muddy to a road at the end - this hike has a little of everything

Sota Sæter to Nørdstedalseter

25.4 km 15.8 miles	1,333 meters 4,373 feet	1,065 meters 3,493 feet	10-12 hours Very Challenging

The day starts with a climb up to a ridge overlooking Sota Sæter, the longest climb on the route. There's about 850 meters of elevation gain before you hit the top of the ridge. After the climb, you'll start to go along the Illvatnet (-vatnet translates to "the lake") in very rocky terrain. This section is very slow going since you'll be scrambling over rocks - there's also limited or no cell phone service in this section. Eventually, you'll clear the rocky section and start the hike down towards Nørdstedalseter, passing a smaller lake used for hydroelectric power. Eventually, you reach the cabin on a construction road.

My hiking notes:

 Especially on the way up, take plenty of breaks. The view behind you is the most impressive view, so turn around and check it out when you need to catch your breath. This is an absolutely spectacular hike, one of my favorites of all time, but it's tough.

The hosts at Nørdstedalseter know that this is a long hike and will serve dinner until late. If you arrive after 10pm or so, you might need to make your own dinner in the self-service cabin attached to Nørdstedalseter, but you won't have to go hungry.

Two tactical tips - screenshot the weather forecast before you leave Sota Sæter. There is no phone service at Nørdstedalseter. The other is not to get confused by some signs saying "Nørstedalseter" and others saying "Nørdstedalseter". UT.no and DNT use both spellings.

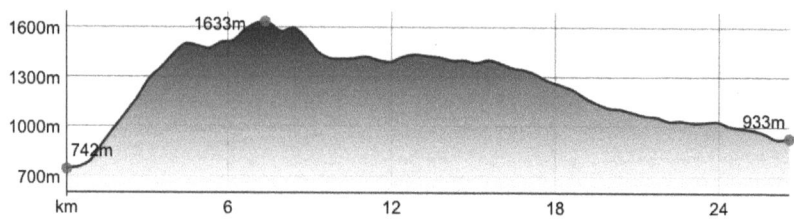

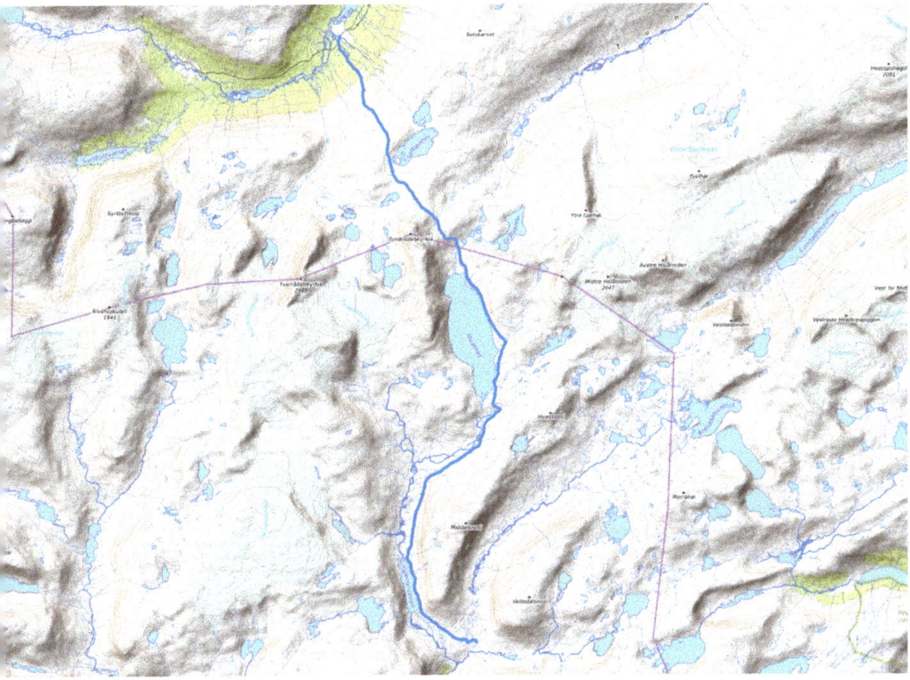

This hike might get my vote for the most spectacular hike in Norway - very tough, very worth it!

Nørdstedalseter to Sognefjellshytta

| 26.5 km | 959 meters | 570 meters | 10-12 hours |
| 16.4 miles | 3,146 feet | 1,871 feet | Very Challenging |

The trail starts out climbing up Vetledalen on a construction road. Pass the trail that turns off towards Stølsdalen and continue along the road, then continue to the northeast on the north side of a lake, Nedre Grønevatnet. Continue climbing all the way up to Tverrbyttfjellet at 1,571 meters above sea level. Depending on snow melt, you may need to wade over a river in this section. After reaching Tverrbyttfjellet and going around the Liabrevatnet,, you'll turn towards the southeast. The trail becomes much rockier through this area, and there will often be snowfields into August.

The trail starts to go towards the west of Storevatnet, a large body of water (literally, the name means "the big water"). It is very rocky through this section and will be very difficult if it's rained. Eventually, the trail towards the east and starts to climb along the front of the dam at the southern end of Storevatnet. From here, the trail climbs slightly, then turns towards the south and drops down to Sognefjellshytta on dirt trails.

My hiking notes:

This one is a doozy. I made the mistake of doing it on a day with pouring rain and freezing fog, and it may have been the toughest hike of my life. I built a lot of character, but I wouldn't do it in that kind of weather again. Especially if you're tired, you might want to wait a day at Nørdstedalseter if the forecast isn't great. The pictures looked spectacular, but I only saw the insides of clouds.

You get up to high elevation during the day, so make sure to have your layers handy. I ended up using a hat and socks on my hands when I did it, even before the weather turned. There will also be snow fields until late in the summer here.

On the good news side - Sognefjellshytta has a buffet dinner that goes until nine at night, so you'll get fed even if you get there late.

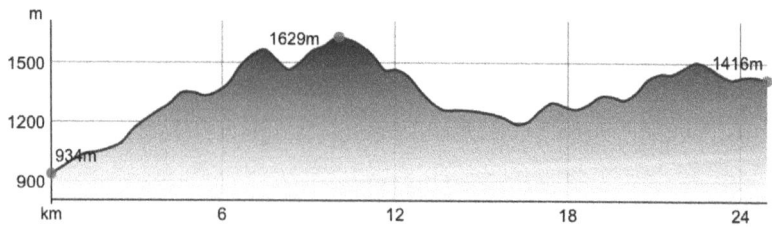

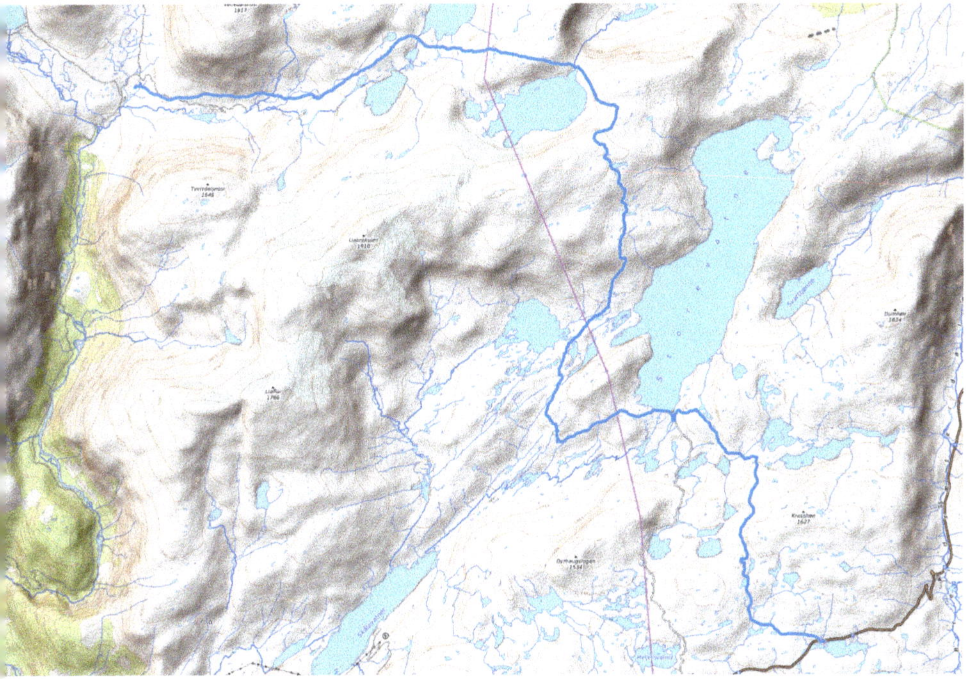

Check out the big water in this picture!

Nørdstedalseter to Trulsbu

15.4 km **9.5 miles**	↗ **563 meters** **1,847 feet**	↘ **219 meters** **718 feet**	 **6 hours** **Challenging**

The hike starts following a construction road from Nørdstedalseter towards Medalsbu (marked on some maps as Middalsbu). At the end of the construction road, about nine kilometers of hiking, there's a sign and then a trail over a rocky portion to Medalsbu. It's about half an hour of walking over rocks and past some small lakes to Medalsbu. Medalsbu is an emergency shelter locked with the DNT key. It's a good spot to sit and have a snack.

From Medalsbu, the hike continues through a rocky section with views all around until it reaches Trulsbu. There are several sections here that may have snowfields left until late in the summer.

<u>My notes</u>

This is a beautiful hike, especially if the weather is good. You can also do it as a day hike from Nørdstedalseter, going just to Medalsbu and then heading back. If you do that, you may also be able to borrow bikes to do the construction road portion of the hike - ask at the reception desk at Nørdstedalseter.

Trulsbu is a beautiful cabin in a fantastic location, but it can be a bit difficult to loop it into a multiday hike because of its location. The T-marked trails from Trulsbu go either to Nørdstedalseter or out of the national park to Bismo. There is a non-DNT marked trail to Sota Sæter, but it goes over a glacier and in more technically challenging terrain.

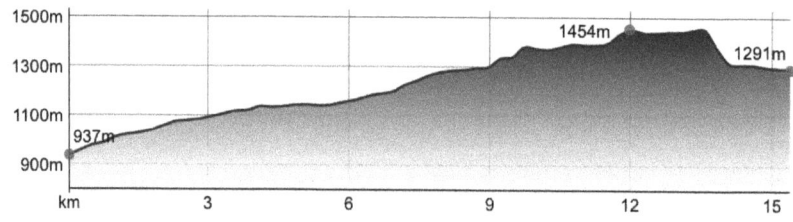

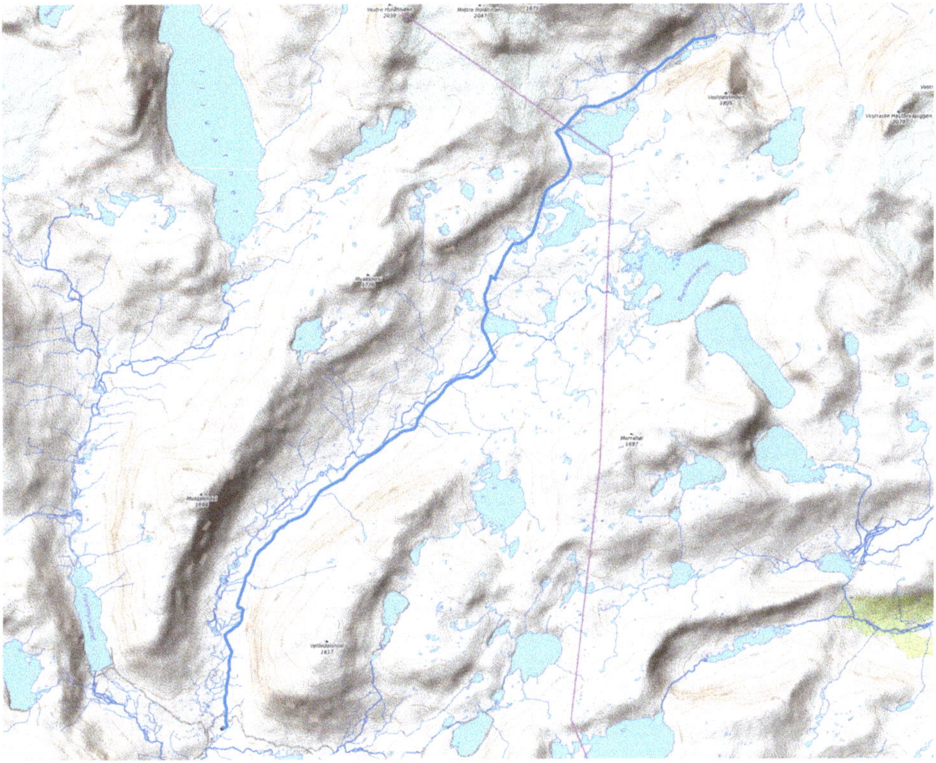

29

Trulsbu to Bismo

| 20.2 km | 129 meters | 648 meters | 5 hours |
| 12.6 miles | 423 feet | 2,125 feet | Moderate |

The trail starts next to Trulsbu and descents down along a river. Note that the trail marked on UT has not been updated as of summer 2024 and is located on the incorrect side of the river; the newly marked trail is on the south side of the river. The trail drops elevation until it reaches the Lundadalsvatnet, where it goes along the south side of the river. The portion next to the lake is almost five kilometers of hiking, so it is substantial. After the end of the lake, the trail crosses through some wetlands and then goes along the north side of the river for almost ten additional kilometers. Here, there is a bridge that crosses over the river, then the trail continues on the south side. Follow the trail on the south side until you reach the parking lot at the end of Lundadalsvegen.

My route notes

There is no phone service on this route, and it's twelve kilometers from the parking lot at Lundadalsvegen to Bismo. If you plan to do this hike and don't have a car, you will want to book a taxi in advance. The taxis in Bismo also don't run on the weekends unless you've booked in advance.

This is a full day hike to get in or out of Breheimen. I underestimated the sheer length of this portion when I did it, and I didn't mentally prepare for what a long day it would be. If you're looking for an easier way to get out of the national park, I'd recommend taking a taxi from Sota Sæter.

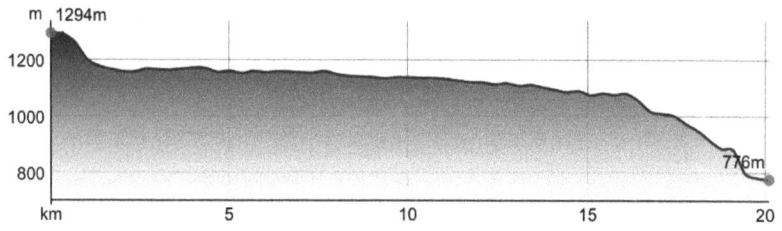

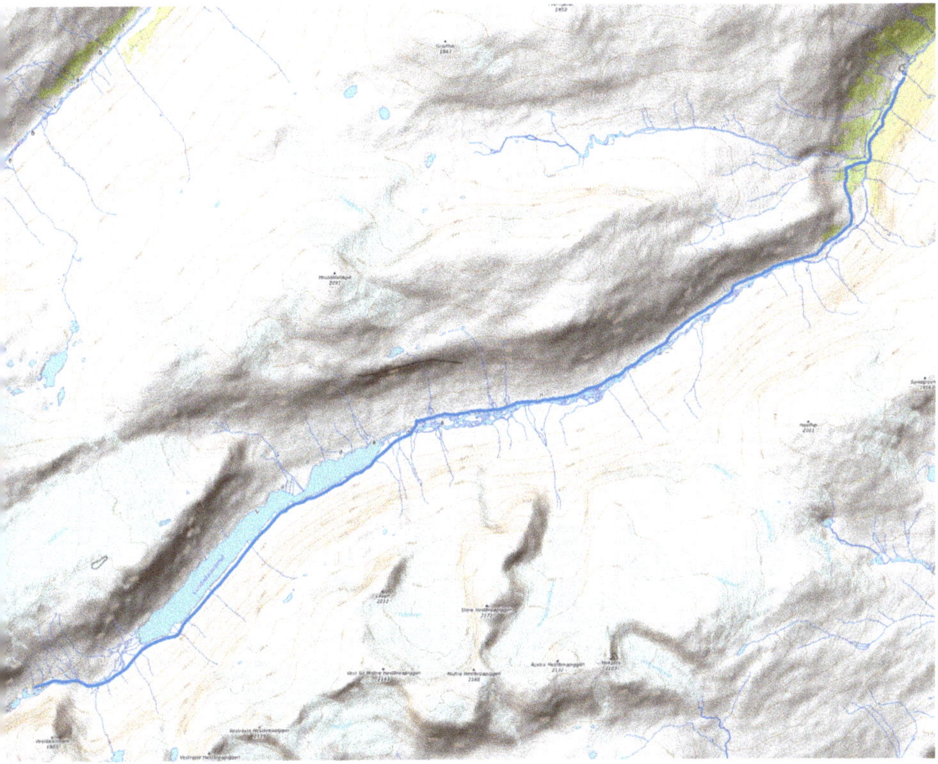

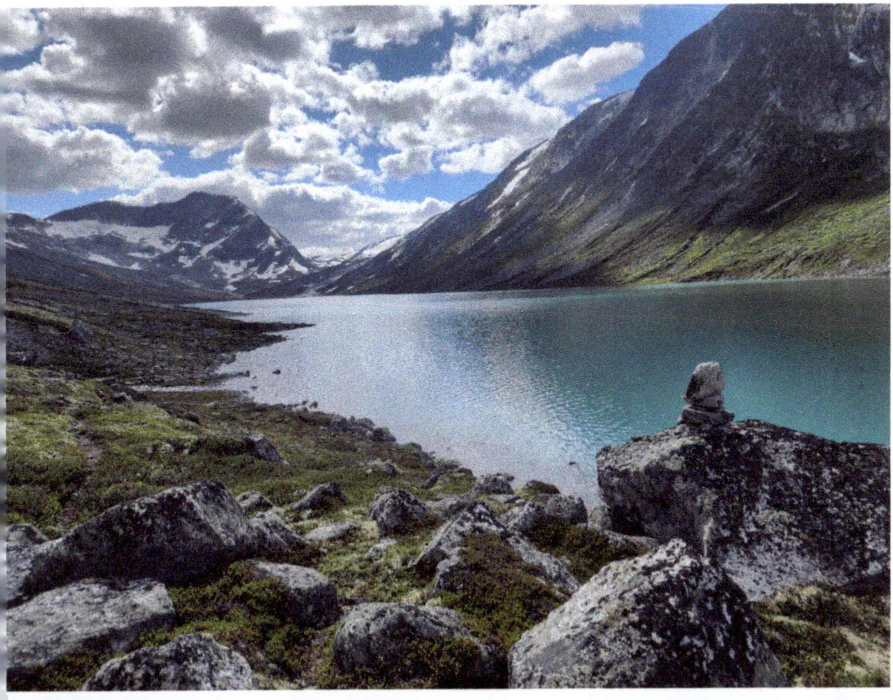

Sprongdalshytta to Slæom

| 21.5 km | 473 meters | 641 meters | 8 hours |
| 13.4 miles | 1,551 feet | 2,103 feet | Challenging |

The trail starts by going north of the lake behind Sprongdalshytta, passing the turnoff for the trail to Arentzbu. From there, the trail climbs slightly up to about 1,350 meters over sea level before starting a descent through a bowl. It's moderately rocky through this section and can have snowfields left. The trail drops steeply down, then turns towards the north and passes by several small lakes. At about 8.5 to 9 kilometers, the trail turns towards the east, passing above Surtbyttvatnet. Continue following the trail until it reaches the intersection with the trail heading to Slæom.

Here, turn towards the west to take the trail towards Slæom. The trail runs along the south side of the river and then along the south side of the Mysubyttvatnet. In case of heavy rain, the rivers past Mysubyttvatnet will need to be waded across.

My notes

This hike isn't too rocky, and you can also split it up in the middle by going to Sota Sæter and spending the night. The middle of the day is especially easy - it can be muddy, but it's much flatter and less rocky than the sections before and after.

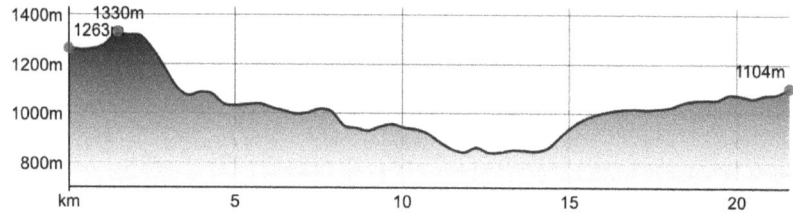

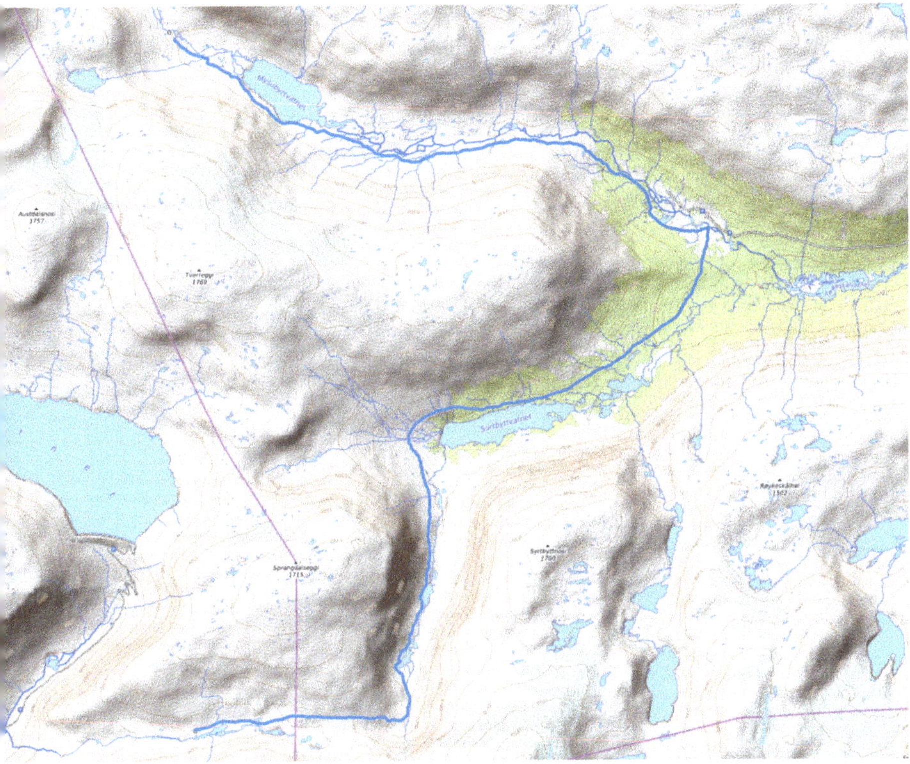

1757
Syrbyttvatnet
1715
1700
1502

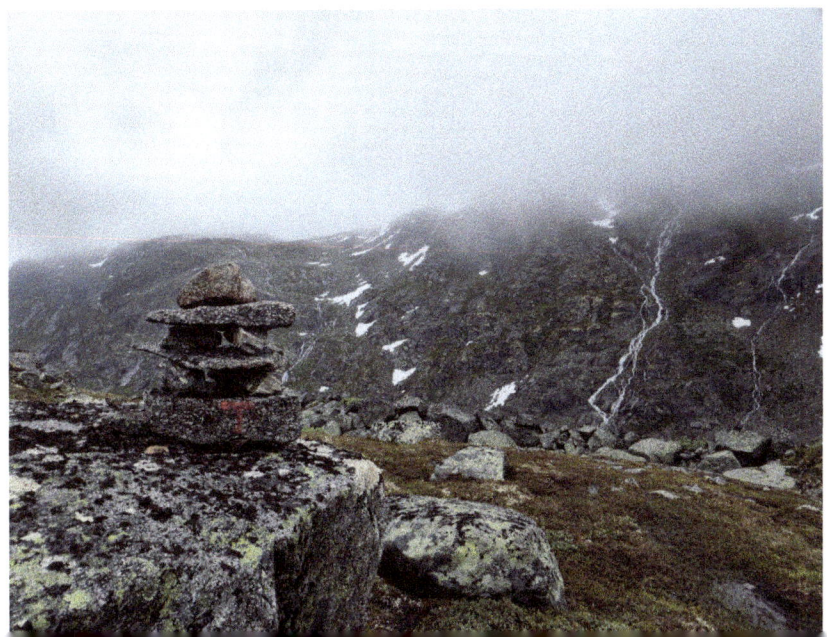

Slæom to Skridulaupbu

| 17.4 km | 747 meters | 938 meters | 9 hours |
| 10.8 miles | 2,450 feet | 3,077 feet | Very challenging |

The trail starts on the north side of the Mysubyttvatnet and then climbs steeply up. Continue to follow the trail up in sometimes rocky terrain until there is a crossing south of a lake at 1,389 meters above sea level. Wade across the river here, then continue to climb up to the next lake towards the northeast, then to the edge of Seekebreen (Seeke glacier).

Go along the edge of the glacier towards the north, climbing up to 1,776 meters. From here, the trail goes in between two glaciers, then begins to drop elevation and head northeast towards Nedre Leirvatnet. Once the trail reaches Nedre Leirvatnet, it's a flat walk to Skridulaupbu close to the western edge of Rauddalsvatnet.

My notes

I had originally planned to do this route and was unable to complete it due to new snow in July. Others I spoke to reported that it was an extremely tiring, difficult route, especially if the weather was rainy or foggy. If you plan to do it, check senorge.no to make sure there isn't new snow, and make sure to have a backup plan in case the weather doesn't cooperate.

There is no phone service along the route, and the closest phone service is 6km away from Skridulaupbu.

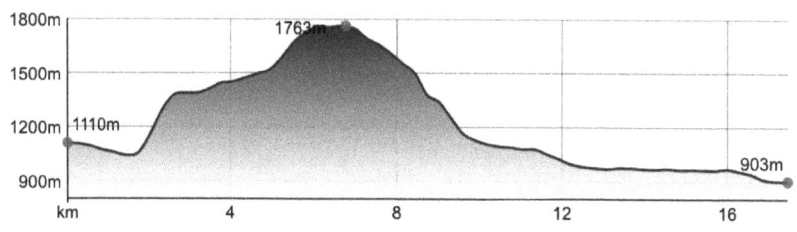

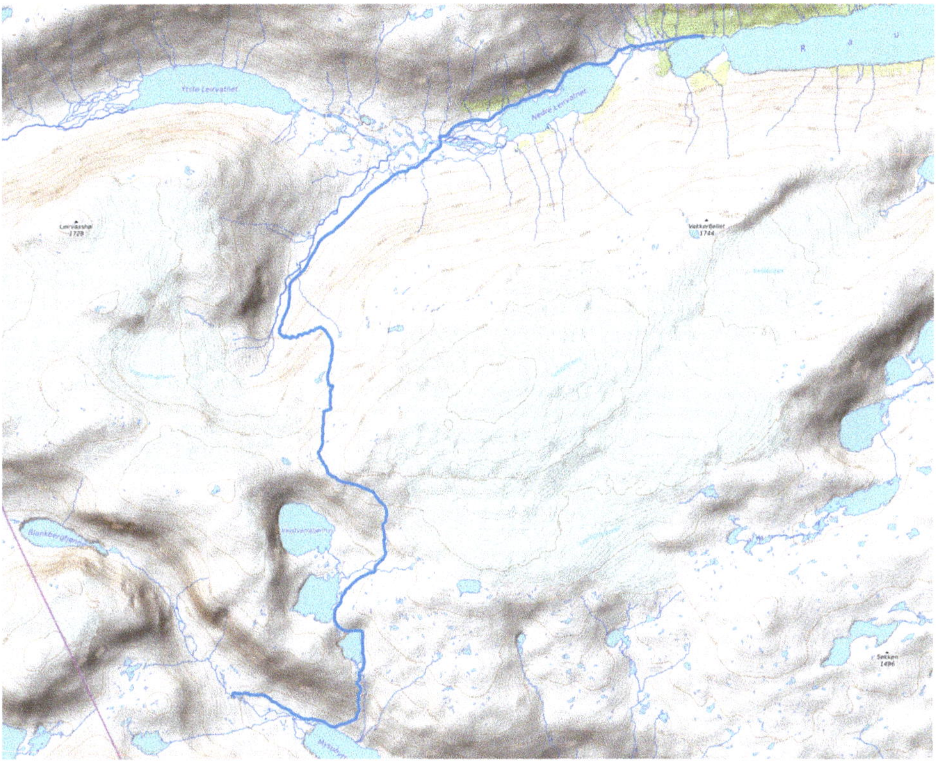
Nedre Leirvatnet
Vakkerfjellet
1744

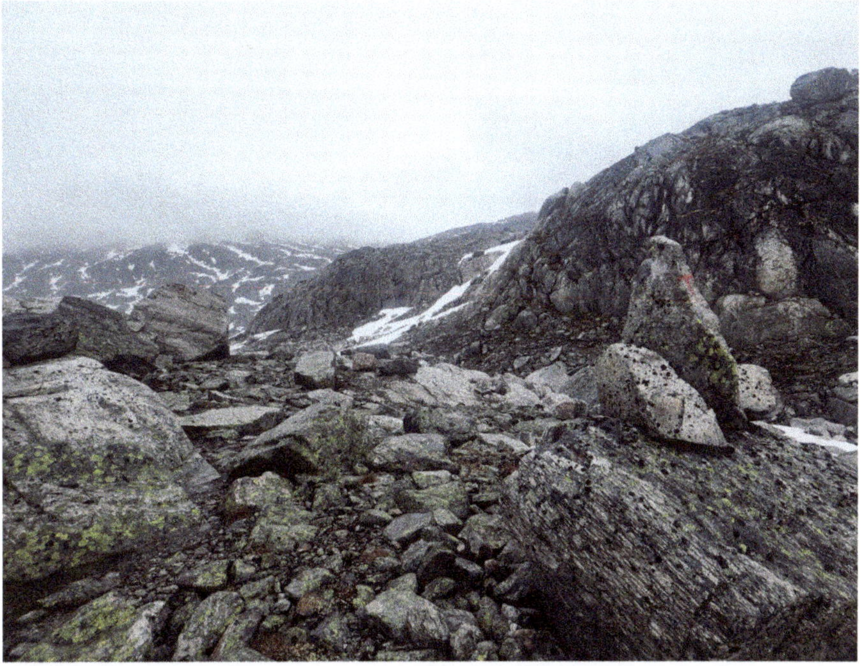

Skridulaupbu to Grotli

| 17.4 km | 821 meters | 838 meters | 9 hours |
| 10.8 miles | 2,693 feet | 2,749 feet | Very challenging |

The trail starts going along Rauddalsvatnet (Raud valley lake) for five kilometers. This section is flat. After this, the trail turns towards the north and begins a steep climb up towards northern Rauddalsåi, a peak. The trail continues past a small lake at 1,477 meters above sea level, then drops slightly as it reaches an intersection. There's a trail towards Sota Sæter here towards the east, but continue north towards Grotli. Eventually, the trail reaches a patch of cabins, then goes through that patch of cabins to FV 258, a road. Follow FV 258 until you reach RV 15, a larger regional road, which goes to Grotli.

My notes

Grotli is a good location for entering Breheimen, but this hike is quite tough and has snowfields into late in the summer. If you're planning a trip in July, check senorge.no for the latest snow conditions and consider starting or ending your hike at Sota Sæter instead.

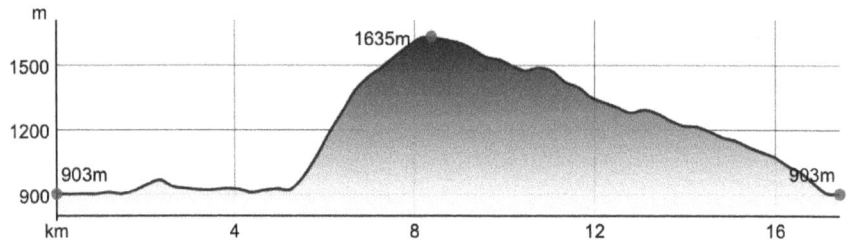

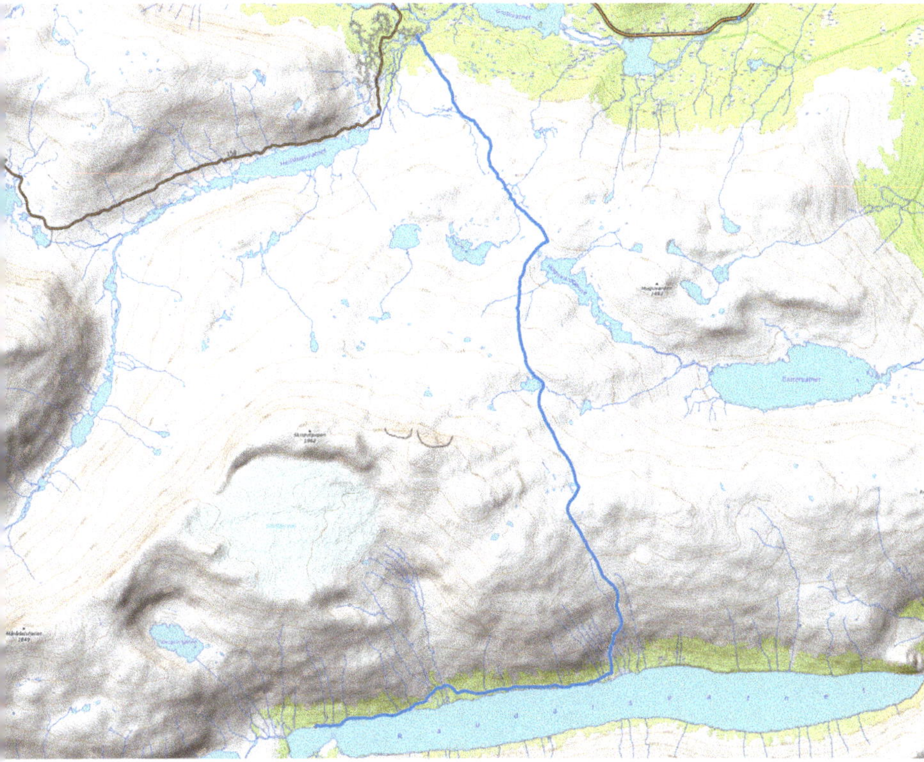

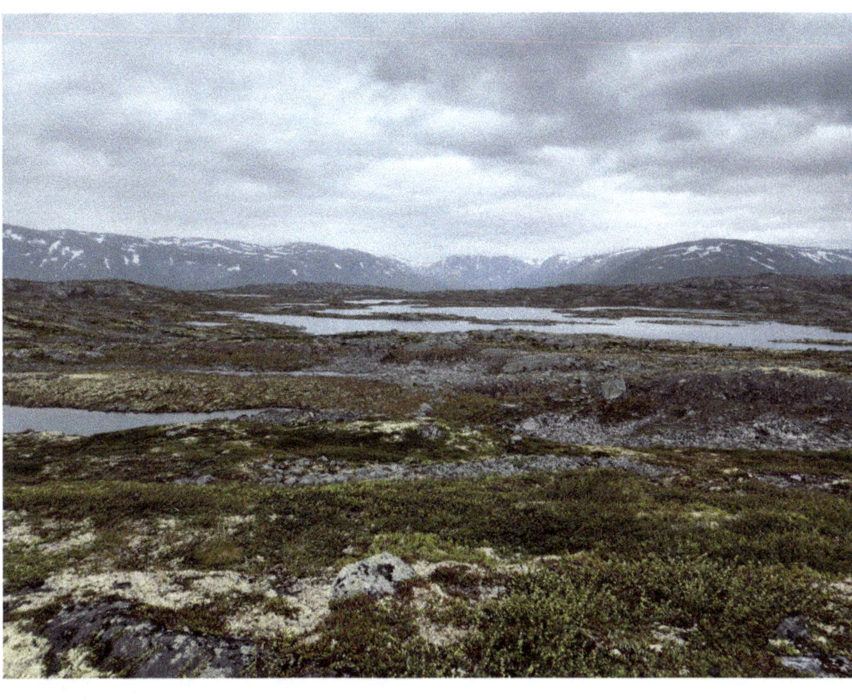

Logistics

Getting There and Back

There are a few spots in Breheimen where you can drop to get to public transport. I recommend Navarsete, Sota Sæter, or Sognefjellshytta as the best entry points. Grotli, Sota Sæter, and Sognefjellshytta are the only cabins that are reachable with public transportation, while Nørdstedalseter, Navarsete, and Fast are reachable with public transit and a 2-3 hour hike. I would not recommend Grotli as a starting point, since the hikes south from Grotli can be extremely difficult during bad weather or early in the hiking season.

- Arentzbu: inaccessible other than by foot. The closest road is a 6-7 hour hike away

- Fast: a 2-3 hour hike from the nearest parking lot, which is located in Mørkri at the back of the Mørkridalen.

- Fivla: the closest parking lot is located above Øvre Vigdal in Vårstølen. After that, it's a 1-2 hour hike to the cabin. There is no public transportation to the parking lot.

- Grotli: The hotel is located on FV15, a major road, and a public bus stops by the cabin at least twice a day. Check entur.no for the exact routing.

- Navarsete: a 2-3 hour hike from the nearest town. You can take the bus to either Gaupne or Høyheimsvik from Sogndal and then hike 2-3 hours to reach Navarsete.

- Nørdstedalseter: there is a gravel road up to the cabin from Fortun. Fortun is reachable with a public bus from Oslo, and after that, a taxi or bike up to the cabin.

- Skridulaupbu: inaccessible other than by foot. Nearest drop point is at Grotli, a minimum 7 hours hike away

- Slæom: inaccessible other than by foot. The closest road is at Mysubuttseter, which is a three hour hike from the cabin.

- Sognefjellshytta: there is a public bus between Otta and Lom that goes two or three times a day during the summer. Check entur.no for the latest schedules.

- Sota Sæter: there is bus service from Oslo to Skjåk, then a minibus service to Sota. Check Sota's website or enTUR for the latest bus routing information. The minibus typically only runs 3-4 days a week, so call Skjåk Taxi if you are arriving on a day without minibus service.

- Sprongdalshytta: inaccessible other than by foot. The closest road is at Viva in the Sprongdal, about 1-2 hours from the cabin. There is no public transit to Viva and very limited phone service.

- Trulsbu: inaccessible other than by foot. The closest public transit is at Sota Sæter, and the closest drop point is at Bismo, a 5-6 hour hike.

- Vigdalstøl: same as Fivla

Supplies

All the cabins in this book, other than Fivla, are self-service or fully serviced cabins, meaning they have food and basic supplies for purchase. Other than the cabins, there are no spots to get supplies within Breheimen. If you need to purchase anything, you'll need to leave the area, take the bus to Sogndal, Lom, or Skjåk, and then start hiking again.

Camping

Norway has some of the most permissive laws in the world around camping. Norway has a law called the Allemannsretten that guarantees the ability of people to explore and experience nature, even in privately owned areas. Once you're in the wilderness, you may camp in any area, as long as you're at least 150 meters away from the nearest inhabited house or cabin, which includes DNT cabins.

Campfires are prohibited everywhere in Norway from April 15 to September 15, except in specifically marked areas in camping sites and by the coast.

All that being said, Breheimen is one of the harder national parks to camp in because so many of the areas are rocky and not comfortable for camping. Breheimen is also known for being colder and more rainy than other parts of Norway. Most of the hikers I've met on my hikes in Breheimen use only the cabins and don't bring a tent. The hikers I met who had a tent all planned to stay in the cabins the majority of the trip and only camp a couple nights.

Packing List

In total, the gear below should weigh between 15 and 25 pounds (7 to 12 kilograms).

Gear

☐ 46-55 liter hiking backpack with a rain shield

☐ Maps and compass

☐ Hiking poles: *I strongly recommend poles for Breheimen. They're extremely useful on snowfields*

☐ Duct tape

☐ Dry bags for packing

☐ Vindsekk, or emergency bivvy: *the weather is very cold and rainy here, so I strongly recommend having a backup bivvy in case you are stuck outside.*

Clothing

☐ Hiking boots: *I recommend high hiking boots given the amount of rock hopping*

☐ Trail runners: *I used these for the less technical hikes to give my feet a break (Gaupne to Navarsete, Trulsbu to Bismo)*

☐ Rain pants and optional gaiters

☐ Rain jacket

☐ Windbreaker: *it's frequently misting in the mornings, so if you don't like hiking in your rain jacket, bring a lighter weight jacket to hike in*

☐ Wool socks, two pairs

☐ Hiking pants or long underwear to layer under rain pants

☐ Wool sweater

Clothing Continued

☐ Extra warm jacket

☐ Two sports bras and two pairs of underwear

☐ Hat and gloves: *it's cold enough you may need these, especially on days with high elevation*

☐ Two hiking shirts

Cabin Supplies

☐ Mini towel

☐ DNT key: *all the cabins in Breheimen are locked with the standard DNT key*

☐ Sengetøy (sheet set) or sleep liner: *required for the cabins*

☐ Toilet shoes: *most of the cabins have outdoor toilets*

☐ Sleep mask: *there are good curtains in the cabins, but it never gets dark*

Food and Drink

☐ Thermos for hot drinks

☐ Small plastic water bottle: *there are plenty of rivers and streams to fill up a water bottle as you're hiking in Breheimen*

☐ Candy and snacks

☐ Plastic bag for sandwiches

Tech

- [ ] Phone: *there's very limited phone service, so expect to keep your phone on airplane mode. I recommend downloading UT, YR, and Hyttebetaling before your hike*

- [ ] Battery pack: *there's no power at Navarsete, Vigdalstøl, or Fast.*

- [ ] Chargers: *many of the cabins only have USB classic charging outlets. If you have a phone with a USB-C charging port, you will want to bring a USB to USB-C charger*

Other

- [ ] Passport and ID

- [ ] Credit cards and backup card

- [ ] Toiletries: *wilderness wash, face wash, toothpaste, toothbrush, contacts, contact lens solution, glasses, hairbrush, hair ties, nail clippers, any medications you take as needed*

- [ ] Tiny shovel and toilet paper

- [ ] First aid kit

- [ ] Extra plastic bags

Some Handy Norwegian Words

Almost all Norwegians speak perfect English. That said, there are times where it's handy to be able to read signs, the weather, or the map.

Hiking and the map

Bratt/meget bratt: steep/very steep

Breen: the glacier

Dalen: the valley

Grusvei: a gravel path

Luftig: steep drop offs on the side of the trail

Kvistet: marked (used for ski trails)

Merket: marked (used for summer trails)

Mobildekning: phone service

Myr: a swampy, wet land covering

Nord, sor, ost, vest: north, south, east, west

Skog: forest

Stein: rocky

Steinur: rocky patches to hike over

Tind/tinden: peak

Vadested: a place that requires wading

Vannet: the water

Varder: cairns

Vatnet: the lake

Vegen: the road

Weather

Bris: breeze

Flom: flood

Lettskyet: barely cloudy

Lyn: lighting

Nedbør: precipitation

Nysnø: new snow (no icy cover yet)

Regn: rain

Weather continued

Skyet: cloudy

Snø: snow

Sol: sun

Soloppgang, solnedgang: sunrise, sunset

Strynregen: very heavy rain

Tåkete: foggy

Torden: thunder

Things in provision rooms

Bønnemix: mixed beans

Erter: peas

Fullkorn: whole grain

Gryte: stew

Hermetikk: shelf-stable boxes

Kaffe: coffee

Kanel: cinnamon

Kokemalt: coffee that needs to be cooked in a kettle

Kjeks: biscuits

Kjøtt: meat

Knekkebrød: crispbread

Kokk uten lokk: cook without a lid

Kylling: chicken

Lapskaus: a Norwegian stew of potatoes and meat

Legg til: add to (e.g. "legg til vann" = "add water")

Linser: lentils

Melkepulver: milk powder (reconstitute with water)

Ost: cheese

Pannekake: pancakes

Food continued

Potetmos: mashed potatoes

Rein: reindeer

Ror godt: stir well

Smør: butter

Sodd: a high calorie stew of pork, potatoes, and some vegetables

Sukker: sugar

Svine: pork

Syltetøy: jam

Turmat: dehydrated hiking food

Vann: water

Cabins

Betjent: serviced (a lodge)

Selvbetjent: self-service (a cabin without staff but with a provision room)

Ubetjent: unserviced (a cabin with beds, propane, and wood, but no food)

Drikkevann: drinking water

Forhåndsbestilt: booked in advance

Hyttefelt: a collection of cabins

Protokoll: the book you have to sign when you arrive at a cabin

Using the Cabins

One of the most amazing things about hiking in Norway is the national cabin network. The Norwegian Trekking Association (DNT) maintains a network of more than 600 cabins spread across the country. It makes it easy to travel deep into the wilderness without carrying food or a tent.

Cabins come in three grades:

Betjent (serviced):

These aren't cabins but full lodges. You'll have a three course meal for dinner, a buffet breakfast with a place to fill your thermos, showers and drying rooms for clothes, and often indoor toilets.

Dinners are served family style, where the staff will bring out giant tureens of soup for a first course, then usually some kind of meat and potatoes, then individual desserts. There's more than enough food for everyone - but make sure to book ahead and alert the cabin if you're vegetarian or have dietary restrictions.

The family style dinners mean that you have to go to an assigned dinner time, usually seven o'clock. There's usually assigned seating as well, and people are generally very excited to chat.

Serviced cabins have electricity but may only have outlets in the common areas, so don't rely on an overnight charge for your devices.

Selvbetjent (self-service)

Self-service cabins are unique to Norway. They're generally smaller than staffed cabins, but come fully stocked with a provisions room, wood for the fireplace, gas for cooking, and cooking supplies. Some have electricity, but it's usually from a single solar panel and is only enough to charge one or two phones. You usually have to fetch and boil water from a nearby water source.

You can unlock any self-service cabin in Breheimen with the DNT key. You can purchase the key at a physical DNT store in Norway, online at their web store, or at a staffed cabin. Payment is on the honor system – use the Hyttebetaling app. The app allows you to keep a list of all the supplies you've used and then pay with credit card when you get back into phone service.

Ubetjent (unserviced)

These are just like self-service cabins, except that there isn't food available in the provision room. Fivla is the only unserviced cabin in Breheimen.

Cabin Etiquette:

When you arrive at an unserviced or self-service cabin, the first thing to do is to unlock the cabin and then take off your shoes. No outdoor shoes are allowed in the cabin to help keep it clean. After that, fill in your information in the besøksprotokoll, a horizontal blue book that asks where you came from, where you're going, and your membership information. After that, you have the right to use the cabin. I generally first start a fire if the cabin is cold, then fetch water to heat up for dinner.

When you leave the cabin in the morning, you'll need to clean up. That means washing all of the dishes, cleaning out the ashes in the fireplace, bringing in fresh wood for the fire, washing the floors in the bedroom and common areas, and any other tidying.

If you're camping and want to stop in and use the cabin, you'll still have to register in the besøksprotokoll and pay for a day visit ("dagsbesøk"). Make sure to sweep up and wash the floors after yourself.

Booking:

It's not necessary to book in advance for any of the cabins in Breheimen - if you arrive at the cabin, you'll have a place to sleep, though it might be on a mattress on the floor if it's really busy. I generally don't book cabins in advance so that I have the most flexibility possible to change hiking plans based on the weather.

Most self-service cabins are open all year round, but some may close during the winter or spring if they're in avalanche prone terrain or in reindeer breeding ground. UT.no will have information on cabin opening times.

Joining DNT:

You'll need to join DNT in order to get the DNT key. There are instructions on how to do that on the blog, or you can go by any DNT office in Norway.

Cooking at the cabin:

There is a propane stove and plenty of cooking supplies in the cabins. The food that you'll generally find breaks down into four categories:

Breakfast: knekkebrød, oatmeal mixes, pancake mix, leverposti (liver spread), jam and chocolate spread, mackerel in tomatoes, butter, jam, and honey

Dinner: fish soup, peas and carrots, mashed potato mix, lapskaus, rice, bacalo, boxed mixes for Pasta di Parma and Chili Con Carne, pasta, reindeer meatballs, dry red lentils, and crushed tomatoes

Snacks and dessert: chocolate pudding, vanilla sauce, canned fruit in syrup, and biscuits

Misc things: dried hiking food, coffee, tea, hot chocolate, currant drink mix, hiking snacks like knekkebrød sandwiches, sugar, cinnamon

Each cabin has a different selection of food, and if you're late in the season, certain items might be eaten up. There's always enough food, but it might not be what you're craving. If you're vegetarian or gluten-free, make sure to have your own backup food.

It can be hard to find something to bring for lunch the next day. I really load up on breakfast at the self-service cabins, often mixing vanilla sauce or jam into my oatmeal for the extra calories. I take two or three packages of freeze dried food with me for backup lunches. Since Breheimen is mostly self-service cabins, you might also consider bringing along some of your own food for some variety. I like pesto and parmesan cheese, as well as other cheese and sausage.

Cabin Overview

Cabin	Cabin Type	Total beds	Number bookable	
Navarsete	Self-service	9	4	
Vigdalstøl	Self-service	10	4	
Fast	Self-service	11	4	
Fivla	Unserviced	24	20	
Arentzbu	Self-service	22	9	
Sprongdalshytta	Self-service	12	4	
Nørdstedalseter	Serviced	42	42	
Trulsbu	Self-service	12	4	
Sota Sæter	Serviced	86	86	
Sognefjellshytta	Private hotel	80	80	
Slæom	Self-service	18	9	
Skridulaupbu	Self-service	4	2	
Grotli	Private hotel	120	120	

Power	Phone Service	Drying Room	Shower
N	Y	N	N
N	N	N	N
N	N	N	N
N	N	Yes, with fireplace	N
N	N	N	N
Yes, 12 volt	N	N	N
Yes, 220 volt	N	Yes, full drying room	Y
Yes, 12 volt	N	N	N
Yes, 220 volt	Y	Yes, full drying room	Y
Yes, 220 volt	Y	Yes, full drying room	Y
Yes, 12 volt	N	N	N
N	N	N	N
Yes, 220 volt	Y	N	Y

Planning Resources

yr.no is the best resource for weather in Norway. It allows you to hike by specific cabin or mountaintop, with the weather for that particular point rather than the overall area. It's available in English.

Senorge.no shows the current and historic weather conditions for any point in Norway. It's very useful for checking the amount of snow remaining for summer hikes.

ut.no is both an app and a website showing all the cabins and trails in Norway. It's unfortunately only in Norwegian, but is the best source of information on cabins and trails. You can download offline maps by going to "Profil" and then "Mine offline-kart" on the app.

Varsom.no is key for the winter and shows storm and avalanche warnings. It's available in English.

If you're stopping by a DNT office before going hiking, you can pick up a planleggingskart, or planning map. These aren't usable for hiking but are great for planning, since they show the locations of cabins and DNT cabins.

Fjellvettreglene (Norwegian Mountain Code)

The Norwegian Mountain Code contains the guidelines for having a safe trip in the Norwegian mountains. They're considered an important part of Norwegian cultural heritage and were introduced after a spate of fatal accidents in 1950.

1. Plan your trip and inform others about the route you have selected.

2. Adapt the planned routes according to ability and conditions.

3. Pay attention to the weather and the avalanche warnings.

4. Be prepared for bad weather and frost, even on short trips.

5. Bring the necessary equipment so you can help yourself and others.

6. Choose safe routes. Recognize avalanche terrain and unsafe ice.

7. Use a map and a compass. Always know where you are.

8. Don't be ashamed to turn around

9. Conserve your energy and seek shelter if necessary.

In case of emergency, notify the police at 112. You can also call 911 or 999, and the dispatch will connect you to the correct service. Within the cabins, there are signs giving the coordinates of the cabins and the emergency numbers.

Sarah Rowe has solo hiked more than 3,500 kilometers across 21 countries, with a focus on Norway and Austria. When she's not out in the mountains, she's drinking coffee, writing about hiking on her blog, Solo Female Wanderer, or planning the next adventure. She lives in the northeastern United States, two kilometers from the Appalachian Trail.

Questions or comments? You can reach her at
sarah@solofemalewanderer.com.